HEALING OUR HEARTS AND LIVES

Inspirations for
Meditation and Spiritual Growth

Edited by

EILEEN CAMPBELL

HarperSanFrancisco

A Division of HarperCollins*Publishers*

First published in the United States of America in 1995
by HarperCollins*Publishers*

*Healing Our Hearts and Lives: Inspirations for Meditation
and Spiritual Growth*. Copyright © 1995 by Eileen Campbell.
All rights reserved. Printed in Great Britain.
No part of this book may be used or reproduced in any
manner whatsoever without written permission except
in the case of brief quotations embodied in critical
articles and reviews. For information address
HarperCollins*Publishers*, 10 East 53rd Street,
New York, NY 10022.

Library of Congress Cataloging-in-Publication Data:
Healing our hearts and lives: inspirations for meditation and
spiritual growth/edited by Eileen Campbell.
p. cm.
Includes bibliographical references.
ISBN 0-06-251323-0 (alk. paper)
1. Spiritual life—Quotations, maxims, etc. 2. Spiritual
healing—Quotations, maxims, etc. I. Campbell, Eileen
BL624.H379 1995
158'.12—dc20 95-6134
CIP

ISBN 0-06-251323-0

95 96 97 98 99 UKA 10 9 8 7 6 5 4 3 2 1

This edition is printed on acid-free paper that meets the
American National Standards Institute Z39.48 Standard.

INTRODUCTION

Healing is a process of becoming more whole, as is clear if we look at the origin of the word 'heal'. The Old English root is 'hal', to make whole, to bring together. We long for wholeness, but all too often feel split, separated, alienated. We all have to deal with healing our hearts and lives, for none of us escapes pain and suffering. Healing our hearts and lives is also a lifelong process, and is a first step towards healing our relationships, our communities and our world.

Where do we begin in this process of healing? Our starting-point must be with our own thoughts. Beyond them there is very little that we can control in our lives. We can work on our attitude by focusing on what is positive, uplifting and inspiring. It is our responsibility to make our lives better for ourselves, and ultimately for others.

We can let nature help to heal us. Through beauty and wonder, through silence and solitude, we can get in touch with something beyond our own egos and feel connected to the source of all life.

We also need to let go of the past. If hurts and disappointments are not acknowledged and healed, we do not live in harmony. Forgiveness of ourselves and others, through compassion, opens the heart, which is the only place where lasting peace is to be found.

We need to be brave, shaking off fear, particularly in times of change and transformation, and we need to have the courage truly to live our lives. Once a sense of meaning and purpose is found, our souls are nourished.

In the process of healing ourselves, we are better able to help heal others. As the shamans have always known, the wounded healer heals.

This anthology, as with my previous books, has been gathered from a wide range of sources, from both East and West. I hope it may prove helpful in the healing process.

Growing whole is a spiritual endeavour. When we expand our awareness, strengthen our centre, clarify our purpose, transform our inner demons, develop our will, and make conscious choices, we are moving toward deeper connection with our spiritual Self, or Spirit – however we name it. Wholeness and spirituality are intertwined.

MOLLY YOUNG BROWN

Everyone should know that you can't live in
any other way than by cultivating the soul.

Apuleius

The beginning of health
is to know the disease.

MIGUEL DE CERVANTES

The natural healing force within each one
of us is the greatest force in getting well.

HIPPOCRATES

Nature, time and patience are
the three great physicians.

CHINESE PROVERB

...we usually think of health as nothing more than the absence of disease. We lack a science of wholeness, of spiritual health.

Sam Keen

The great malady of the twentieth century, implicated in all of our troubles and affecting us individually and socially, is 'loss of the soul'. When soul is neglected, it doesn't just go away; it appears symptomatically in obsessions, addictions, violence, and loss of meaning. Our temptation is to isolate these symptoms or to try to eradicate them one by one; but the root problem is that we have lost our wisdom about the soul, even our interest in it.

THOMAS MOORE

Healing is discovering how to live life in trust rather than in fear, how to relate to life as friend rather than enemy. It is about falling in love with life, learning to listen and respond to the longing impulses of the heart because these alone guide us to realize life's intention for us.

ANNE BARING

The physician should know the invisible as well as the visible man. There is a great difference between the power which removes the invisible cause of disease and that which merely causes external effects to disappear.

PARACELSUS

The most divine art is that of healing. And if the healing art is most divine, it must occupy itself with the soul as well as the body; for no creature can be sound so long as the higher part of it is suffering.

PYTHAGORAS

One of the basic principles of holistic health is that we cannot separate our physical body from our emotional, mental, and spiritual states of being. For instance, when we have a physical disorder, it is a message for us to look deeply into our emotional and intuitive feelings, our thoughts and attitudes, to discover how we need to take better care of ourselves emotionally, mentally, or spiritually, as well as physically. With this approach we can restore the natural harmony and balance within our being.

SHAKTI GAWAIN

There is an Indian proverb or axiom that says that everyone is a house with four rooms, a physical, a mental, an emotional, and a spiritual. Most of us tend to live in one room most of the time but, unless we go into every room every day, even if only to keep it aired, we are not a complete person.

RUMER GODDEN

Healing does not necessarily mean to become physically well or to be able to get up and walk around. Rather, it means achieving a balance between the physical, emotional, intellectual, and spiritual dimensions.

ELISABETH KÜBLER-ROSS

You ought not to attempt to cure eyes without head, or head without body, so you should not treat body without soul.

SOCRATES

...the purpose of healing is to bring us in harmony with our earth, with our environment, and with ourselves.

O. CARL SIMONTON

We cannot separate the healing of the individual from the healing of the planet. They are one and the same, because the consciousness of each individual is connected to the collective consciousness. Although we are individuals, we are also each a part of the whole. As we begin to heal ourselves as individuals, we also naturally shift the consciousness of the entire planet. And as the collective consciousness begins to shift, we are each in turn affected by it. Thus, the more people change their consciousness and their way of life, the more the world changes; and the more the world changes, the more individuals change.

SHAKTI GAWAIN

HEALING OUR
HEARTS AND LIVES

But what is a man profited if he gains the whole world and loses his own soul? Or what will a man give in exchange for his soul?

MATTHEW 16:26

You know of the disease in Central Africa called sleeping sickness... There also exists a sleeping sickness of the soul. Its most dangerous aspect is that one is unaware of its coming. That is why you have to be careful. As soon as you notice the slightest sign of indifference, the moment you become aware of the loss of a certain seriousness, of longing, of enthusiasm and zest, take it as a warning. You should realize your soul suffers if you live superficially.

ALBERT SCHWEITZER

Your soul is your life. Everything else is a fiction – a mind game, in authenticity. Without nourishing your own soul, you can't nourish the world; you can't give what you don't have. As your soul grows, however, it emanates invisibly and involuntarily the light which it has received.

RICHARD CARLSON AND

BENJAMIN SHIELD

When we create peace and harmony
and balance in our minds, we will
find it in our lives.

LOUISE L. HAY

Healing the heart is about cherishing in every sense: cherishing the time given to us in order to discover who we truly are; cherishing the body; cherishing the lives of the people who have been given into our care; cherishing the planetary life which is the great field of all our endeavours.

A N N E B A R I N G

The first step toward planetary healing is to walk toward the beauty in thee – to see the beauty in your own heart, to forgive those ideas and correct those thought forms that obscure the true wisdom fire in your mind.

DHYANI YWAHOO

First keep the peace within yourself,
then you can also bring peace to others.

THOMAS À KEMPIS

Acceptance, inclusion, and integration are the keys to wholeness. No part of us, no matter how repugnant, gets thrown out. Every aspect has value and truth. As soon as we reject or deny any part of ourselves, we are fragmented. Wholeness means exactly that: no part left out.

MOLLY YOUNG BROWN

We are not unified; we often *feel* that we are, because we do not have many bodies and many limbs, and because one hand doesn't usually hit the other. But metaphorically, that is exactly what does happen within us. Several sub-personalities are continually scuffling: impulses, desires, principles, aspirations are engaged in an unceasing struggle.

ROBERTO ASSAGIOLI

We must steadfastly practise peace, imagining our minds as a lake ever to be kept calm, without waves, or even ripples, to disturb its tranquillity, and gradually develop this state of peace until no event of life, no circumstance, no other personality is able under any condition to ruffle the surface of that lake or raise within us any feelings of irritability, depression or doubt ... and though at first it may seem to be beyond our dreams, it is in reality, with patience and perseverance, within the reach of us all.

DR EDWARD BACH

What is it you need when you're down? A helping hand. You need good thoughts inside of you to counterbalance the bad thoughts. And you'd better have an arsenal of affirmations that can pick you up out of any situation and straighten you out and get you going.

JOHN-ROGER

Your mind will be like its habitual thoughts:
for the soul becomes dyed with the
colour of its thoughts.

▬▬▬

MARCUS AURELIUS

We are all immersed in the atmosphere of our own thinking, which is the direct result of all we have ever said, thought or done. This decides what is to take place in our lives. Thought attracts what is like itself and repels what is unlike. We are drawn toward those things which we mentally image.

ERNEST HOLMES

We can accent in ourselves absolutely everything which exists. What is accentuated is elevated into being the dominant element and in the long run transforms all the other elements in conformity with its proper character … no state exists which cannot, by conversion, disruption, or remoulding of the personality, be abruptly changed into a completely different state.

HERMAN KEYSERLING

One's own thought is one's world.
What a person thinks
is what he becomes –
That is the eternal mystery.
If the mind dwells
within the supreme Self,
One enjoys undying happiness.

MAITRI UPANISHAD

There is one great obstacle that keeps us from knowing the Self, and that is the mind. The mind veils the inner Self and hides it from us. It makes us feel that God is far away and that happiness must be found outside. Yet the same mind that separates us from the Self also helps us to reunite with it. That is why the ancient sages, who were true psychologists, concluded that the mind is the source of both bondage and liberation, the source of both sorrow and joy, our worst enemy as well as our greatest friend. That is why, if there is anything worth knowing in this world, it is the mind.

SWAMI MUKTANANDA

Your happiness depends on three things, all of which are within your power: your will, your ideas concerning the events in which you are involved, and the use you make of your ideas.

EPICTETUS, A MANUAL FOR LIVING

Your mind will say things to you, and then your eyes will start to look around for whatever it is that your mind says you lack. Then your emotions start to follow that, the feelings start to hurt, the body grabs a hold of it, and pretty soon you're sick.

So now you know how to be sick, and you know how to make yourself even sicker. Yet you can reverse that. You do it by watching where you put your eyes. Watch where you put the feelings as they come up. Put your emotions where you want your body to go. These are very simple directions for just living life.

▬

JOHN-ROGER

Happiness and freedom begin with a clear understanding of one principle: some things are within your control, and some things are not. It is only after you have faced up to this fundamental role and learned to distinguish between what you can and can't control that inner tranquility and outer effectiveness become possible.

EPICTETUS, A MANUAL FOR LIVING

We have a choice then. Seeking beauty
becomes in great part our responsibility.
We can be exposed to what Assagioli called
'psychic smog' – the prevailing mass of
free-floating psychological poisons – or turn
instead to the healing influence of beautiful
sights and sounds.

PIERO FERRUCCI

Peace of mind is the key to healing. The experience we call peace is the physical/emotional perception of being in God's presence, feeling at One with the source of our being.

JOAN BORYSENKO

The emphasis on true mental healing is insistently on God, the One Mind, the One Soul, the One Being, ever-present and ever-available; and on man's ability and right to make himself receptive to this healing Presence – a realization of the essential divinity of our own nature, and the truth that no evil can live in this Presence. We must unify ourselves with the great whole.

ERNEST HOLMES

Every moment of your life is infinitely creative and the universe is endlessly bountiful. Just put forth a clear enough request, and everything your heart desires must come to you.

Ask, and it shall be given you; seek, and ye shall find; knock, and it shall be opened unto you.

For everyone that asketh receiveth; and he that seeketh findeth; and to him that knocketh it shall be opened.

MATTHEW 7:7,8

You begin to see that God cannot give and God cannot withhold. You can shut yourself off from the grace of God, but through prayer you can be reunited with your Source. Your prayer will not be a seeking for any thing; it will be an asking and a knocking for more light, greater spiritual wisdom, greater discernment.

JOEL GOLDSMITH

He who can believe himself well,
will be well.

OVID

Try to keep your mind constantly on the pleasant aspects of life and on actions which can improve your situation. Try to forget everything that is irrevocably ugly or painful. This is perhaps the most efficient way of minimizing stress.

HANS SELYE

Everything can be taken from a man but one thing: the last of human freedoms – to choose one's attitude in any given set of circumstances, to choose one's own way.

VICTOR FRANKL

Peace of mind is clearly an internal matter. It must begin with your own thoughts, and then extend outward.

It is from your peace of mind that a peaceful perception of the world arises.

A COURSE IN MIRACLES

Me as I think I am and me as I am in fact – sorrow, in other words, and the ending of sorrow. One third, more or less, of all the sorrow that the person I think I am must endure is unavoidable. It is the sorrow inherent in the human condition, the price we must pay for being sentient and self-conscious organisms, aspirants to liberation, but subject to the laws of nature, and under orders to keep on marching, through irreversible time, through a world that is wholly indifferent to our well-being, towards decrepitude and the certainty of death. The remaining two-thirds of all sorrow is home-made and, so far as the universe is concerned, unnecessary.

ALDOUS HUXLEY

What really frightens and dismays us is not
external events themselves, but the way in
which we think about them. It is not things
that disturb us, but our interpretation of their
significance.

EPICTETUS, A MANUAL FOR LIVING

We either make ourselves miserable, or we make ourselves strong. The amount of work is the same.

CARLOS CASTANEDA

The fountain of content must spring up in the mind; and he who has so little knowledge of human nature as to see his happiness by changing anything but his own disposition, will waste his life in fruitless efforts, and multiply the griefs which he proposes to remove.

SAMUEL JOHNSON

A Sage was once asked, 'What is the way to respond to pain and discontent in our lives?' She answered, 'There are those who will meet sorrow and pain as an enemy. Raging at the world, they will find someone to blame, thinking only in terms of fault and blame. There are those who will bewail their fate, saying, "What have I done to dèserve this, why am I so unlucky?" There are those who will blame themselves. Succumbing to guilt, they will believe that their very worthlessness deserves the punishment of suffering. There are also those who will meet pain and discontent not as an enemy but as a teacher. They will follow the path of the wise, asking, "What is the root of this sorrow? What is the path to healing and what will I learn from this moment?" '

CHRISTINA FELDMAN

Healing takes place as our minds become
attached to the truth of our Being.

ERNEST HOLMES

Therefore let us inculcate in ourselves and in our children the means of achieving mental and spiritual health. By this I mean let us teach ourselves and our children the necessity for suffering and the value thereof, the need to face problems directly and to experience the pain involved.

M. SCOTT PECK

Every disease is a doctor.

———

IRISH PROVERB

Much of your pain is self-chosen.
It is the bitter potion by which the physician
within you heals your sick self.
Therefore trust the physician, and drink his
remedy in silence and tranquillity.

KHALIL GIBRAN

MACBETH: Cans't thou not minister to a mind
diseas'd,
Pluck from the memory a rooted
sorrow,
Raze out the written troubles of
the brain,
And with some sweet oblivious
antidote
Cleanse the stuff'd bosom of that
perilous stuff
Which weighs down upon the
heart?

DOCTOR: Therein the patient
Must minister to himself.

WILLIAM SHAKESPEARE

MACBETH V.III.40–6

The world breaks everyone and afterward
many are strong at the broken places.

ERNEST HEMINGWAY

When an emotional injury takes place, the body begins a process as natural as the healing of a physical wound. Let the process happen. Trust that nature will do the healing. Know that the pain will pass and, when it passes, you will be stronger, happier, more sensitive and aware.

MELBA COLGROVE

So you must not be frightened ... if a sadness rises up before you larger than any you have ever seen; if a restiveness, like light and cloud-shadows, passes over your hands and over all you do. You must think that ... life has not forgotten you, that it holds you in its hand; it will not let you fall. Why do you want to shut out of your life any agitation, any pain, any melancholy, since you really do not know what these states are working upon you? Why do you want to persecute yourself with the question whence all this may be coming and whither it is bound? ...just remember that sickness is the means by which an organism frees itself of foreign matter; so one must just help it to be sick, to have its whole sickness and break out with it, for that is its progress ... you must be patient as a sick man ... there are in every illness many days when the doctor can do nothing but wait. And this it is that you, in so far as you are your own doctor, must now above all do.

RAINER MARIA RILKE

Our most difficult experiences become the crucibles that forge our character and develop the internal powers, the freedom to handle difficult circumstance in the future and to inspire others to do so as well.

STEPHEN R. COVEY

Through the practice of silence we become aware of our pain. The pain is always there – in our minds and in our bodies. Silence allows us to see it, face it, release it.

GUNILLA NORRIS

Help is here.

Learn to be quiet in the midst of turmoil, for quietness is the end of strife and this is the journey to peace.

A Course in Miracles

If you bring forth what is within you, what you bring forth will save you. If you do not bring forth what is within you, what you do not bring forth will destroy you.

THE GOSPEL OF THOMAS

Disease is a kind of consolidation of a mental attitude, and it is only necessary to treat the mind of a patient and the disease will disappear.

DR EDWARD BACH

One thing I have learned is that attitudes should not be underestimated in any assessment of the healing equation.

Reshape yourself through the power of your will; never let yourself be degraded by self-will. The will is the only friend of the Self, and the will is the only enemy of the Self.

EKNATH EASWARAN

BHAGAVAD GITA 6:5

We must accept finite disappointment,
but we must never lose infinite hope.

MARTIN LUTHER KING

In the midst of winter, I finally learned that there was in me an invincible summer.

ALBERT CAMUS

Hope is the thing with feathers
That perches in the soul,
And sings the tune without the words,
And never stops at all.

EMILY DICKINSON

When a little bubble of joy appears in your sea of consciousness, take hold of it and keep expanding it. Meditate on it and it will grow larger. Keep puffing at the bubble until it breaks its confining walls and becomes a sea of joy.

PARAMAHANSA YOGANANDA

Follow your bliss.

JOSEPH CAMPBELL

A good mind, a good heart, warm feelings –
these are the most important things. If you
don't have such a good mind, you yourself
cannot function. You cannot be happy, and so
also your own kin, your own mate or children
or neighbours and so forth won't be happy
either.

THE FOURTEENTH DALAI LAMA

I go to Nature to be soothed and healed,
and to have my senses put in tune once more.

JOHN BURROUGHS

You must converse much with the field and woods, if you would imbibe such health into your mind and spirit as you covet for your body.

HENRY DAVID THOREAU

There is something infinitely healing in the repeated refrains of nature – the assurance that dawn comes after night, and spring after winter.

RACHEL CARSON

Our aspirations are our possibilities.

ROBERT BROWNING

The pessimist sees the difficulty in
every opportunity; the optimist the
opportunity in every difficulty.

L. P. JACKS

What we vividly imagine, ardently desire,
enthusiastically act upon,
must inevitably come to pass.

COLIN P. SISSON

A rockpile ceases to be a rockpile the moment
a single man contemplates it, bearing
within him the image of a cathedral.

ANTOINE DE SAINT-EXUPÉRY

...we do not need research to know that the magnificence of a cathedral's rose window, the design of Celtic manuscripts, a flower in full bloom, or the perfect geometry of a Greek temple does not leave us unaffected. And the moment we let ourselves be touched by beauty, that part of us which has been badly bruised or even shattered by the events of life may begin to be revitalized. At that moment a true victory takes place – victory over discouragement, a positive affirmation against resigning ourselves to the process of crystallization and death. That victory is also a step forward in our growth in a very precise and literal sense, for the moment we fully appreciate beauty we become more than we were. *We live a moment of pure psychological health.* We effortlessly build a stronghold against the negative pressures that life inevitably brings.

PIERO FERRUCCI

Where there is no vision,
the people perish.

PROVERBS 29:18

Enthusiasm is the yeast that makes your hopes rise to the stars. Enthusiasm is the sparkle in your eyes, the swing in your gait, the grip of your hand, the irresistible surge of will and energy to execute your ideas.

HENRY FORD

Paradise is nearer to you than
the thongs of your sandals.

THE KORAN

A human being has the freedom to become anything. By his own power he can make his life sublime or wretched. By his own power he can reach the heavens or descend to the depths. In fact, the power of a human being is so great that he can even transform himself into God. God lies hidden in the heart of every human being, and everyone has the power to realize that.

SWAMI MUKTANANDA

Affirmation of life is the spiritual act by which man ceases to live unreflectively and begins to devote himself to his life with reverence in order to raise it to its true value. To affirm life is to deepen, to make more inward, and to exalt the will-to-live.

ALBERT SCHWEITZER

It is not because things are difficult that we do not dare; it is because we do not dare that they are difficult.

S E N E C A

To try is to risk failure. But risk must be taken because the greatest hazard of life is to risk nothing. The person who risks nothing does nothing, has nothing, is nothing. He may avoid suffering and sorrow, but he simply cannot learn, feel, change, grow, live and love.

LEO BUSCAGLIA

One of the most tragic things I know about human nature is that all of us tend to put off living. We are all dreaming of some magical rose garden over the horizon – instead of enjoying the roses that are blooming outside our windows today.

DALE CARNEGIE

Risk! Risk anything! ...
Do the hardest thing on earth for you.
Act for yourself. Face the truth.

You never live so fully as when you
gamble with your own life.

ANTHONY DE MELLO

We must be willing to get rid of the life we've planned, so as to have the life that is waiting for us. The old skin has to be shed before the new one can come.

JOSEPH CAMPBELL

To have courage for whatever comes in life –
everything lies in that.

SAINT TERESA OF AVILA

Every year I live I am more convinced that the waste of life lies in the love we have not given, the powers we have not used, the selfish prudence that will miss nothing, and which, shirking pain, misses happiness as well.

MARY CHOLMONDELY

You have the power to heal your life, and you need to know that. We think so often that we are helpless, but we're not. We always have the power of our minds. Do you use your mind to think of yourself as a victim? Do you walk around feeling mad at yourself, or complaining about others? Do you feel as though you have no power to do anything about changing your life? This is giving your power away. Your mind is a powerful tool. Claim and consciously use your power. You have the power to choose to see things working out for the best. Recognize that you are always connected with the One Power and Intelligence that created you. Feel and use this support. It is there.

LOUISE L. HAY

Nothing in life is to be feared.
It is only to be understood.

MARIE CURIE

Disease is an experience of so-called mortal mind. It is fear made manifest on the body.

MARY BAKER EDDY

Fear imprisons, faith liberates; fear paralyses,
faith empowers; fear disheartens,
faith encourages; fear sickens, faith heals;
fear makes useless, faith makes serviceable.

HARRY EMERSON FOSDICK

Be strong and of good courage;
be not frightened, neither be dismayed...

JOSHUA 1:9

God is our refuge and strength, a very present help in trouble. Therefore will we not fear, though the earth be removed, and the mountains be carried to the midst of the sea.

PSALM 46:1–2

If you are distressed by anything external, the pain is not due to the thing itself but to your own estimate of it; and this you have the power to revoke at any moment.

MARCUS AURELIUS

If we are truly in the present moment, and not being carried away by our thoughts and fantasies, then we are in a position to be free of fate and available to our destiny. When we are in the present moment, our work on Earth begins.

RESHAD FEILD

Our remedies oft in ourselves do lie.

WILLIAM SHAKESPEARE

ALL'S WELL THAT ENDS WELL I.I.235

We are healed from suffering only
by experiencing it to the full.

PROUST

Call the world, if you please,
'the vale of Soul-making'.
Then you will find out the
use of the world.

JOHN KEATS

Let your mind be quiet, realizing the beauty of the world, and the immense, the boundless treasures that it holds in store.

EDWARD CARPENTER

Silence is our deepest nature, our home,
our common ground, our peace.
Silence reveals. Silence heals.

GUNILLA NORRIS

The important thing is not to think too much,
but to love much; and so do that which
best stirs you to love.

ST TERESA OF AVILA

You will forget your misery; you will
remember it as waters that have
passed away.

JOB 11:16

All healing is release from the past.

A Course in Miracles

Let not the sun go down upon your wrath...

Let all bitterness, and wrath, and anger, and clamour, and evil speaking, be put away from you, with malice;

And be ye kind one to another, tenderhearted, forgiving one another, even as God for Christ's sake hath forgiven you.

PAUL'S EPISTLE TO THE EPHESIANS
4:26, 31–2

I believe that all genuine healing addresses
the problem of unblocking negativities
in one way or another.

———

SUN BEAR

The world is ruled by letting things take their course. It cannot be ruled by interfering.

LAO TZU

The main reason for healing is love.

PARACELSUS

...the common denominator of all healing methods is unconditional love – a love that respects the uniqueness of each individual client and empowers the client to take responsibility for his or her own well-being.

JACK SCHWARZ

All healing involves replacing fear with love.

A COURSE IN MIRACLES

You are a child of the universe, no less than the trees and the stars; you have a right to be here. And whether or not it is clear to you, no doubt the universe is unfolding as it should. Therefore be at peace with God, whatever you conceive Him to be.

MAX EHRMANN

When you can forgive both another and yourself ... you move from the law of karma (action and reaction) into the law of grace (resolution) – that effulgent state that transmutes and heals.

BRUGH JOY

The only thing that is going to save people and save the world is if we forgive and love each other. It doesn't mean that I have to like everything that you have done. But not to forgive means that there are things that I can't forgive myself for either. Everything is forgivable once one understands why people are the way they are.

BERNIE SIEGEL

Forgiveness is the answer to the child's dream of a miracle by which what is broken is made whole again, what is soiled is again made clean.

DAG HAMMARSKJÖLD

Oh my servants, who have been too harsh with your souls, with yourselves, despair not the mercy of God, for God forgives all sins.

THE KORAN

...genuine forgiveness is participation, reunion overcoming the powers of estrangement... We cannot love unless we have accepted forgiveness, and the deeper our experience of forgiveness is, the greater is our love.

PAUL TILLICH

To forgive is the highest, most beautiful form of love. In return, you will receive untold peace and happiness.

ROBERT MULLER

One should forgive under any injury. It hath been said that the continuation of the species is due to man's being forgiving. Forgiving is holiness; by forgiveness the universe is held together. Forgiveness is the might of the mighty; forgiveness is sacrifice; forgiveness is quiet of mind. Forgiveness and gentleness are the qualities of the self-possessed. They represent eternal virtue.

MAHABHARATA

May the healing stream of Allah's forgiveness bathe the hearts of all human beings, cleansing every channel in their spiritual bodies from the subtle fire of the negation of love, the rebellion against love, the self-centred distortion of love.

LEX HIXON

Non-forgiveness is rooted in our habit of thinking self-centred thoughts. When we believe in such thoughts, they are like a drop of poison in our glass of water. The first, formidable task is to label and observe these thoughts until the poison can evaporate. Then the major work can be done: the active experiencing as a bodily physical sensation the anger's residue in the body, without any clinging to self-centred thoughts. The transformation to forgiveness, which is closely related to compassion, can take place because the dualistic world of the small mind and its thoughts has been deserted for the non-dual, non-personal experiencing that alone can lead us out of our hell-hole of non-forgiveness.

CHARLOTTE JOKO BECK

Love is all we have, the only way
that each can help the other.

EURIPIDES, ORESTES

Forgiveness is the exercise of compassion and is both a process and an attitude. In the process of forgiveness, we convert the suffering created by our own mistakes or as a result of being hurt by others into psychological and spiritual growth. Through the attitude of forgiveness we attain happiness and serenity by letting go of the ego's incessant need to judge ourselves and others.

JOAN BORYSENKO

Our first duty is not to hate ourselves.

SWAMI VIVEKANANDA

To love yourself is to heal yourself.

A COURSE IN MIRACLES

Nobody out there can love you the way you
want to be loved. Only you can do that.

JOHN-ROGER

The ability to love oneself, combined with the ability to love life ... enables one to improve the quality of life.

DR BERNIE SIEGEL

So how do you love yourself? First of all and most important: cease all criticism of yourself and others. Accept yourself as you are. When you approve of yourself, your changes become positive. Everyone in your world is a reflection of your beliefs. Don't blame others; change your beliefs. Be gentle, kind and patient with yourself. Praise yourself as much as you can.

LOUISE L. HAY

Let each loving relationship that you have with another human being live primarily inside you. If you place it in the world, you will experience difficulty. There is no relationship out there. There is only the reflection of what you are doing inside yourself and how you're dealing with relationships inside of you, not out there.

JOHN-ROGER

To live without forgiveness is to live separated from the sacred and from the most basic instincts of our heart. To live with forgiveness is to reveal in each moment the beauty and value of life. To live with forgiveness is to choose in each moment an active role in creating relationships, organizations, communities, and a world that works for everyone.

ROBIN CASARJIAN

Human pain does not let go of its grip at one point in time. Rather, it works its way out of our consciousness over time. There is a season of sadness. A season of anger. A season of tranquillity. A season of hope.

ROBERT VENINGA

Kinship is healing; we are
physicians to each other.

OLIVER SACHS

To the soul, there is hardly anything
more healing than friendship.

THOMAS MOORE

...the healing process is made up of
unconditional love, forgiveness,
and letting go of fear...

GERALD JAMPOLSKY

...acceptance becomes the quickest and most practical way to free oneself from a difficult situation, while rebellion inexorably tightens the knot.

———

PIERO FERRUCCI

In the spiritual journey, the compass unfailingly points towards compassion. This spiritual compass is the equivalent of the satellite Ground Position System that pilots and ship captains use to discover their exact location. Inscribe this single word on your heart – 'compassion'. Whenever you are confused, keep heading in the direction that leads toward deepening your love and care for all living beings, including yourself, and you will never stray far from the path to fulfilment.

SAM KEEN

The kingdom of heaven is found in the place of your compassion. It's found in the place of your loving. It's found in the place of your generosity. It's found in the place of your healing of yourself and others. It's very easy to find the kingdom of heaven inside.

When we stop using the intellect of the mind and come to the wisdom of the heart, we access the door to Divinity, because out of that heart comes the compassion and forgiveness.

JOHN-ROGER

Acceptance does not mean resignation or even approval; we do not have to give up hope for change. Acceptance is simply a realistic recognition of things being the way they are and a willingness to work from that base. Acceptance is always the first step in healing, as paradoxical as that may seem. We need to work with ourselves and with others from where we actually are now, not from where we would like to be.

MOLLY YOUNG BROWN

He who goes to the bottom of his own heart
knows his own nature; and knowing his
own nature, he knows heaven.

M ENCIUS

All acts of healing are ultimately
our selves healing our self.

RAM DASS

The wise person looks within his heart
and finds eternal peace.

HINDU PROVERB

Peace is not absence of strife. Peace is acceptance and surrender to that which is. Peace is the profound awareness of the one true source from which all things emerge ... and to which all things return.

GUNILLA NORRIS

'There is no peace except the peace of God.' Seek you no further. You will not find peace except the peace of God. Accept this fact, and save yourself the agony of yet more bitter disappointments, bleak despair, and sense of icy hopelessness and doubt. Seek you no further. There is nothing else for you to find except the peace of God.

A COURSE IN MIRACLES

There is no difficulty that enough love will
not conquer; no disease that enough love
will not heal; no door that enough love will
not open...

EMMET FOX

Only love can bring us peace. And the experience of love is a choice we make, a mental decision to see love as the only real purpose and value in any situation.

MARIANNE WILLIAMSON

The soul is made of love and must ever strive to return to love. Therefore it can never find rest nor happiness in other things. It must lose itself in love. By its very nature it must seek God, who is love.

MECHTILD OF MAGDEBURG

Our function is to let our minds be healed, that
we may carry healing to the world, exchanging
curse for blessing, pain for joy, and separation
for the peace of God.

A COURSE IN MIRACLES

You will be made whole
As you make whole.

A COURSE IN MIRACLES

As the human species awakens to itself as a collection of immortal souls learning together, care for the environment and the earth will become a matter of the heart, the natural response of souls moving towards their full potential.

GARY ZUKAV

You understand that you are healed
when you give healing.

A COURSE IN MIRACLES

A healed person is automatically a healer. And his or her strength is the greater for having been through dark times and brought a conscious solution as a gift to the world.

ROBERT A. JOHNSON

Those who are healed become
the instruments of healing.

A COURSE IN MIRACLES

ACKNOWLEDGEMENTS
AND
FURTHER READING

The editor would like to thank the following authors and publishers for permission to reprint material from their books:

Borysenko, Joan, *Guilt is the Teacher, Love is the Lesson* (The Aquarian Press, 1993).

–, *Pocketful of Miracles* (Warner Books, 1994).

Brown, Molly Young, *Growing Whole: Self-realization on an endangered planet* (Hazelden, 1993).

Brussat, Frederic and Mary Ann (eds), *100 Ways to Keep Your Soul Alive* (HarperSanFrancisco, 1994).

Joseph Campbell Companion: Reflections on the art of living, selected and edited by Diane Osbon, (HarperCollins, 1991).

Carlson, Richard, and Shield, Benjamin, *Handbook for the Soul* (Little, Brown, 1995).

Casarjian, Robin, *Forgiveness: A bold choice for a peaceful heart* (Bantam, 1992).

Cousineau, Phil (ed.), *Soul: An Archaeology: Readings from Socrates to Ray Charles* (HarperSanFrancisco, 1994).

Easwaran, Eknath, *Bhagavad Gita* (Nilgiri Press, 1985).

Epictetus (a new interpretation by Sharon Lebell), *A Manual for Living* (HarperSanFrancisco, 1994).

Ferrucci, Piero, *What We May Be: The visions and techniques of psychosynthesis* (Turnstone Press, 1982).

Foundation for Inner Peace, *A Course in Miracles* (Arkana, 1985).

Gawain, Shakti, *Creative Visualization* (Whatever Publishing, 1978).

Goldsmith, Joel, *The Art of Spiritual Healing* (Harper & Row, 1957).

Grof, Christina and Stanislav, *The Stormy Search for the Self: Understanding and living with spiritual emergency* (Thorsons, 1991).

Hay, Louise L., *You Can Heal your Life* (Eden Grove Editions, 1988).

–, *The Power is within You* (Hay House, 1991).

–, *Meditations to Heal your Life* (Hay House, 1994).

Holmes, Ernest, *The Science of Mind* (Dodd, Mead & Co., 1938).

John-Roger, *The Tao of Spirit* (Mandeville Press, 1994).

–, *Forgiveness: The key to the kingdom* (Mandeville Press, 1994).

John-Roger, and McWilliams, Peter, *You Can't Afford the Luxury of a Negative Thought* (Thorsons, 1991).

–, *Life 101* (Thorsons, 1991).

Jones, James W., *In the Middle of this Road We Call our Life: Connecting with your heart's desires* (Harper-SanFrancisco, 1995).

Keen, Sam, *Hymns to an Unknown God: Awakening the spirit in everyday life* (Bantam, 1994).

Keyserling, Herman, *From Suffering to Fulfillment* (Selwyn & Blount, 1938).

Moore, Thomas, *Care of the Soul: How to add depth and meaning to your everyday life* (HarperCollins, New York, 1992).

–, *Soul Mates: Honouring the mysteries of love and relationships* (Element Books, 1994).

Swami Muktananda, *Where Are You Going?: A guide to the spiritual journey* (Guruder Sidda Peeth, Ganeshpuri, printed in the USA, South Fallsburg, 1981).

Norris, Gunilla, *Sharing Silence: Meditation practice and mindful living* (Bell Tower, 1992).

Peck, M. Scott, *The Road Less Travelled: A new psychology of love, traditional values and spiritual growth* (Hutchinson, 1983).

Sardello, Robert, *Facing the World with Soul: The reimagination of modern life* (Lindisfarne Press, 1992).